ZIOI

MW01127755

THE INSPIRATIONAL STORY OF HOW ZION WILLIAMSON BECAME THE NBA'S FIRST DRAFT PICK

By

JACKSON CARTER

CleanCoachingBlog.com

TABLE OF CONTENTS

LEGAL NOTES
Zion Williamson

CHAPTER 1: A CHILD DESTINED TO BE SPECIAL

Mount Zion is a well-known landmark, the highest point in ancient Jerusalem. It is a historical and religious site that holds a special place in many peoples' lives. Lately, however, a different Zion has been capturing the attention of today's society, particularly NBA and basketball fans all over the world. That Zion is Zion Williamson. The anticipated number one overall pick in the upcoming draft, Zion has already found himself on magazine covers, interviews, viral videos, and more. When you browse social media highlight reels, it is likely that you've seen one of his outstanding, advanced dunks, or even see him in an interview speaking like a young man who is truly grateful for every opportunity and ounce of talent he's been given. Just like the biblical landmark, Zion Williamson has found a special place in history, and, it turns out, his name set the tone for the rest of his life.

On July 6, 2000, Zion's mother, Sharonda Sampson, chose the name Zion for her son because her grandmother told her to pick an extra special name. She believed that her great-grandson would need that name because he was going to have a special life ahead of him. Neither of them nor Zion's father, Lateef Williamson, could have known just how right Sharonda's grandmother's intuition was. None of them could have truly known that Zion needed an extra special name because he was going to have an extra special life to go along with it, but after 18 years, it's pretty clear that he does.

Like many stories, Zion's story begins with his family. Zion's mother, Sharonda, was a track athlete, competing in the high jump. She was able to clear the six-foot mark consistently throughout her college career. She also knew what hard work and dedication could get you, and applied those to her studies and athletics at Livingstone College. Zion's father, Lateef, was also athletic. He was a gifted defensive lineman in high school and college, even earning recognition as a 1993 High School All-American. He measured in at 6'4 and 270lbs providing the size and strength that Zion inherited today. He began playing at North Carolina State University but then transferred to Livingstone College.

Sharonda and Lateef met at Livingston College and began dating. After they were married, they started their family. Most people would probably believe that, based on these two parents, any children that they had would be naturally athletic. They would be correct. They welcomed baby Zion, and both their athletic genes and their support have made him into the young man he is today. Even though they divorced and Sharonda remarried, they've been there for him since the beginning, advising him, coaching him, and helping him to maintain a sense of normalcy through it all.

In the beginning, they lived in Salisbury, North Carolina but moved as a family from Salisbury to

Florence, South Carolina after Sharonda's grandmother passed away. Sharonda and Lateef divorced and, when Zion was around 5 years old, Sharonda married Lee Anderson. Lee was another college athlete, a former Clemson basketball player, who played under Bill Foster for three years. He, too, understood what it meant to play at a high level and strive to be the best. In fact, Lee was only weeks away from going to an NBA camp when he was struck by a car. He was devastated. He questioned his faith and asked God and how something so bad could happen to him just before he was on his way to possibly accomplish his goals. In recent interviews, Lee tells that on the way to the hospital in the ambulance, God answered him. He told Lee that the goal that he was striving for wasn't meant for him. Instead, he would be blessed through his children. And when he married Sharonda and Zion showed an interest and affinity for basketball, he realized that it was true. And he poured his love and knowledge into Zion to help Zion achieve his own dream. Lee believes that he was meant to add the final piece that would eventually lead to Zion's burgeoning basketball career.

CHAPTER 2: THE BUDDING OF A DREAM

Together, Zion's family, especially his mother, helped him to grow into a talented youth, but passion and dedication were there from a young age. Paired with this, his parents instilled in him a sense of humility and faith to keep Zion grounded. Like most parents, they were supportive of their child but also knew that his goals and ambitions were more than likely to change over time. They took an active role in his life, coaching and guiding him through any endeavor, whether it was related to a sport or not. They understood the importance of keeping your dreams in check and having college as not only a backup plan but as an essential part of his future. Like many parents, they did their best to support his dreams but also make sure that he was ready to do something else should it not be possible for some reason. They didn't know it yet, but Zion was already displaying some indicators of greatness, even as just a boy.

With all of his parents being former collegiate athletes, it is no surprise that when Zion began to grow, he participated in sports. He actually began playing when he was just five years old. Zion tried both football and soccer, in addition to basketball, which he ultimately chose to pursue on its own. His stepdad, Lee, helped foster that love of basketball, even when he was just a few years old. In fact, at the age of five, Zion actually declared that his goal was to become a star basketball player when he grew up.

Like many children, he was already set on something, even though he had likely a very little indication of what achieving that goal truly meant. He didn't realize at the time that there even was an NBA, he was simply concerned with becoming a college basketball star, number one in the country. Zion couldn't have known at the time that even with parents who played at the college level, becoming a star in a sport is less likely than getting struck by lighting. But, as children do, he set his sights on becoming one of the all-time greats anyways. And when he finally found out about the NBA, his goal didn't change except that now, he wanted to be the best as a pro.

Unlike many young children, though, Zion took action to accomplish the goal that he set for himself. He worked with his stepdad and mother, both who would later play larger coaching roles for him. By the time he was nine, he displayed the discipline that many adults can't even fathom by waking up at 5am every morning to train.

His passion became evident through his work ethic, but also in the way that he approached others that played the game. When he signed up for Amateur Athletic Union (AAU) ball, he played for the Sumter Falcons and his mother was the coach. But he wasn't playing at his own level with other five-year-olds. He wasn't even playing at the level above his age group. In fact, he was playing against other teams who had players that were four years older than Zion, kids who were nine years old! And it wasn't just a fluke, he was able to compete at a level that well-surpassed other kids his age.

His family pushed him to be the best at what he did and his own love of the sport and showmanship developed into a solid passion for basketball. Zion was, even at a young age, obsessed with dunking. He would hound older players about whether they could dunk and then ask and ask for them to show him. This passion and dedication to the sport really showed his family that it wasn't just a passing phase, that Zion was, and is, still very much in tune with his goals to be a star.

Obviously, a five-year-old who can play with and against other teams that are almost twice his age is an indication of the kind of talent and drive that Zion and his family had. His stepdad still talks about how hard Zion worked at that age, working on his ball handling skills and fundamentals until he absolutely shined on the court, no matter who he was playing. It was no surprise, then, that when Zion joined the Johnakin Middle School team in 6th grade, Sharonda coached him again since she was a teacher there as well. And again, it paid off. Their team was so successful, in fact, that they only lost a total of three games in two years.

The average height of an NBA player is 6' 7" and in 8th grade, Zion, however, was only coming in at 5' 10" which could be one of the reasons that he knew that he needed to work that much harder if he still wanted to achieve his goals. He constantly worked on his skills as a point guard. He is left-handed and, with the help of his stepdad, was able to develop his ball-handling skills as well as his ability to shoot from the perimeter as well as drive to the basket. During his middle school career, he averaged 20 points a game and was a noticeable factor on the court.

All of these skills were necessary for someone who wasn't tall enough to be dominant in the paint, but later came in handy in making him a uniquely diverse threat anywhere on the court.

Looking back, Zion recalls that when he was 10 or 11 years old, he reiterated his earlier goals, telling his parents that he wanted to be in the NBA. At this age, he had a much more realistic idea of what that may mean, but still, his family sat him down and talked to him about what that kind of life would look like. For example, there wouldn't be the opportunity to meet with friends and family as he could now. He'd also have to deal with the publicity and lack of privacy that sometimes came along with being in the limelight. Zion's family wanted him to know just how difficult and tiring that kind of life could become, despite all of the fun and excitement of playing basketball on a professional stage. Becoming an NBA player isn't just about being drafted and putting on the jersey, they told him, there were changes that came to that type of lifestyle that could be really difficult to deal with if someone goes into it and is not ready for it. With their combined experiences as collegiate athletes, his family knew exactly what kind of hard work and perseverance Zion would need in order to get there, plus what it could do to you once you arrived. And yet, Zion insisted that he was ready for that.

His maturity at that age and his family's ability to talk to him about the realities of such a future indicate what is probably one of the more underemphasized factors of Zion's success: his upbringing. His family was constantly there supporting him and pushing him to be the best because they didn't just believe in his dream, they believed in him as well. It was that conversation at 10 or 11, that Sharonda remembers a change in Zion. This was the age that he truly didn't just wake up and practice, he started lifting weights and training even harder, vigilant in his pursuit of being the best. And it was at that point that his mother made sure that he kept his feet on the ground, even if he was shooting for the stars.

Looking at the hard work and dedication that the whole family committed to in order to support Zion, it is no surprise that he grew into a humble and dedicated young man. Although he already had a solid grasp on the fundamentals, he wasn't necessarily the standout that he became later in his career. It wasn't until he was a freshman in high school that things really began to change for Zion.

CHAPTER 3: FRESHMAN YEAR

The family moved once again to Spartanburg, South Carolina just before Zion went into high school. Spartanburg is a small town whose area is known predominantly for its football tradition. It is the home of Stephen Davis, former NFL running back, but is generally not known for any standout athletes. Zion attended Spartanburg Country Day School, a K-12 private school that didn't have any real basketball tradition or program. It was also incredibly small. In fact, there were only a total of 450 students (pre-K through 12th grade) and many of the students were from business families. Students were required to participate in at least one sport, helping them to stay well-rounded and provide a basis of teamwork and communication that many sports help to develop.

When looking back on his career, many wondered why he went to that school when there were other, more popular choices for those looking to join strong basketball programs. Sharonda knew that if Zion was going to truly stand out, he was going to run into a lot of publicity and attention, but at a small school that wasn't primarily focused on basketball, Zion would also have a chance at a normal teenage experience. And, despite its lack of a strong basketball tradition, Spartanburg Country Day provided another piece to the growing puzzle of Zion's career: his coach, Lee Sartor.

Lee Sartor was actually a full-time Sheriff's Deputy who had run the school's basketball program for years. However, when Zion came to the school, Zion changed things. For everyone. In fact, the summer before his freshman year, Zion grew from about 5'10" to 6' 3" and put on some weight to go along with the height passing the 200lb mark. It was a summer filled with growing pains, but it turned the tide in his chances for accomplishing his dreams. His stepdad, Lee Anderson, looked at him and told him that he predicted that Zion would be one of the top contenders in basketball by his junior and senior years. This faith in his abilities and skills, plus his growth spurt, gave Zion some confidence but he tried to stay humble and knew that, at the time, he wasn't on anyone's radar. Despite this, the height and confidence gave Zion just enough to finally attempt and succeed at dunking both during practices and warm-ups, but also in games. Now, he's the one who gets asked and wheedled to dunk by children, and when he hears that, he always loves to deliver.

Through his performance on the team during his freshman year, he led the Spartanburg Day Griffins to their first appearance in the South Carolina Independent School Association State Championship Game. He increased his points per game average from his middle school average from 20 points to 24.4 points per game. But, he also added in a rebound average of 9.4, 2.8 assists, 3.3 steals, and 3 blocks per game. Clearly, he was a handy and impactful presence all over the court, on both offense and defense. He was named to the All-Region and All-State teams for his performance. It turns out, his newfound height and the years of hard work and dedication combined pretty nicely. However, excelling in the private school stage was just one part of how his career amped up during his freshman year.

In addition to playing for his school team, he used his height and skills to play for the South Carolina Hornets, another AAU team based out of Columbia. His stepdad, Lee, would help coach him throughout his AAU careers as well. During this time, he played with Ja Morant, who ended up becoming one of the greats at Murray State and is also scheduled to join Zion in the 2019 NBA draft.

Because the AAU team was based out of a city that neither of the two boys lived, they each drove about 45 minutes to attend games and practices for the team. It was through this team that Zion was finally beginning to make a name for himself. Highlight reels of gameplay and mixtapes of his dunks started circulating and Zion's height and ball-handling skills drew a lot of attention. In fact, he was offered his first scholarship while he was still a freshman, from Wofford University. He also finished out the year by being named to and playing in the SCISA North-South All-Star game, which was outstanding accomplishment for his first year in high school.

When interviewed about his success as a young man, Sharonda looks back at those times and reflects on how, as a mother, it can sometimes be hard to see that your child really has the potential to be great. Too often, we look too favorably and in such a biased way that we can't appreciate our children in a subjective way. However, she recalled that there were many times when strangers, people who didn't realize that Sharonda was Zion's mother, would speak about Zion and compliment his skills. They would talk about how they were sure that one day, he'd end up on TV, playing in the NBA. She realized then, that if others were noticing the way he stood out and were hypothesizing greatness, maybe her views of his capabilities weren't out of proportion after all.

The family also did their best to make sure that even though he was shining on the court, he kept a sense of humility about him and never let his emerging fame get the better of him. In fact, Sharonda would only let Zion watch his own highlights twice, once when they were first posted, and a second time when he was having a bad day. This way, he wasn't sitting there glorifying himself or obsessing on the past, he was constantly looking at the present and future instead.

CHAPTER 4: SOPHOMORE YEAR

Moving on to his sophomore year, Zion continued to grow on and off the court. He was now 6' 6" and continued to dominate and grow his self-confidence on the court. He was able to handle the ball and distrubte the ball for assists, but found that when it came to taking on the power forwards and shooting guards who often had to defend him, it was a mismatch, and it was in his favor. His height and skills showed in the increase of his stats for the year, averaging 28.3 points, 10.4 rebounds, 3.9 blocks, and 2.7 steals a game.

Yet again, the awards and the recognition stacked up. This time, he not only got named to the SCISA All-Star game, but he also won the SCISA Player of the Year for his region. Through this, he led Spartanburg Day to their first state championship in the school's history. He was even invited to the National Basketball Players Association Top 100 Camp and ended up being the leading scorer.

He continued to develop his love of dunking, performing advanced windmill and 360-style dunks that helped him win the Under Armour Elite 24 Dunk Contest in New York. And the rest of the basketball community was really beginning to take note of Zion's abilities. In fact, it was in his sophomore year that he began receiving offers from Division 1 schools like Clemson, Florida, and South Carolina. By the end of his sophomore season, he had been approached by a total of 16 universities who wanted to give him scholarships to play basketball at their schools. With the pressure and fame rising, Zion's maturity and level-headedness prevailed. He decided that he would put off the decision on where he would go to college until his senior year and so that he could remain focused on playing to the best of his ability at the level that he was at. Besides, his family still maintained that he should have as normal of an experience as he could have.

Because of his fame on the basketball court, a traditional school setting, packed with thousands of high schoolers could have been overwhelming to Zion. However, because he was at a school where many of the students were more concerned about their own futures, he was able to take advantage of the smaller setting and just be seen as "Zion." This was a welcome relief where he could focus on being a teenager instead of the target of the highlight reels and awards and allowed him to maintain some semblance of normalcy.

Sharonda stated that she chose that school, where the 9-12 population was only about 150 students, because the other students were from families who owned big corporations and were not starstruck or jealous over Zion's abilities, they were able to provide him as unbiased of a peer group as was possible for him. And his family treated him that way as well. Zion's mother would take his phone at night and still sees him as the hungry teenager who raids the fridge at midnight, adding a level of refreshing reality to

Zion's world. He wasn't treated like a star at home or at school, just as another teenager who is doing his best to make it through the rough teenage years. And it shows. In interviews, Zion's down to earth nature and realistic view of his world is heartening, providing a much-needed breath of fresh air to many who follow the basketball community. And his ability to stay present and focused was tested even more when he hit his junior year of high school.

CHAPTER 5: JUNIOR YEAR

This was the year that everything really became different for Zion. His highlight tapes were going viral on YouTube and people who weren't closely tuned into the high school basketball community began to take note of Zion's skills.

This reached a whole new level when the rapper Drake took a picture wearing Zion's Spartanburg Day jersey and posted it to Instagram. This sparked hundreds and hundreds of notifications, messages, and phone calls to Zion's cell, who was surprised when he awoke and found all of them waiting for him on his phone. This was one of those surreal moments for Zion as Drake is his favorite rapper and he didn't realize that someone so famous could know who he was and even go so far as to publicize his jersey. Now, high school basketball jerseys aren't exactly mass manufactured for public purchase, so it was a surprise in more than one way. When asked, Drake replied to Zion that he had had the jersey custom made, adding even more to the complementary aspect of his post.

In addition to Drake, others like Odell Beckham posted pictures wearing his jersey as well. Floyd Mayweather even FaceTimed with Zion and Dez Bryant, Nate Robinson, and Dwight Howard all reached out and sent Zion messages. Zion's name, face, and highlights were making their rounds through pop culture and sports stars alike. NBA All-Star Steph Curry even filmed his reactions to some of Zion's dunk highlight videos. Curry commended Zion on his skills and said that he was "unreal" but took his praise a step further. Curry pointed out Zion's dedication and passion, that those were the intangible, unteachable, aspects of the game that truly made Zion a standout in Curry's opinion. In the preseason, he was named to the 50 Man Naismith Prep Player of the Year watch list and even appeared as the headlining cover image on the June edition of Slam Magazine. Clearly, this was a good year for Zion.

And the changes didn't stop there. People were flocking to Spartanburg Day, some even going so far as to drive for hours to see the games where Zion would play in. In fact, so many coaches were flying in private jets to come and see Zion play, the local airport was close to running out of the room just to handle the traffic. Zion performed for locals and travelers alike. And he put on a show for them. That season, he averaged 36.8 points, 13 rebounds, 3 steals, and 2.5 blocks per game. He broke the state record for the most 30-point games in a season with 27 games, providing fans a lot of game time to see him dominate the floor against a variety of other schools and teams. And by the middle of his season, he broke the 2000 point mark by scoring 48 points against Oakbrook Preparatory School. The Spartanburg Day Griffins even went on to beat Oakbrook later on to win the region championship game that resulted in Zion scoring 37 points in the uneven bout that ended in Oakbrook only scoring 49 points to Spartanburg Day's 105.

A couple of tournament games really bumped his averages as he performed at a level that he hadn't reached before. His stepdad, Lee, commented that the bigger the stage, the bigger Zion will play, and those games were prime examples of that. In the Tournament of Champions, against Proviso East High School, it seemed like Zion was everywhere. He had a 50 point game, with 10 in-game dunks, plenty of and-ones, and 5 blocks. The blocks that are filmed show Zion coming from virtually nowhere and vaulting himself into the air, his head above the rim, as he hammers away layups and jump shots alike.

Thanks to his size, he does well in the paint. Adding in his point guard foundation only makes him a bigger threat. He can move easily through defenders, split a defense in half, and glide through the air to slam it home. Crowds went wild each and every time he crossed someone over, took a fast break in for a windmill dunk, or just finessed his way around the defending centers, who tried a number of strategies trying to cut Zion off, but none were very effective.

In another tournament, the Chick-fil-A Classic, he even broke the tournament record by scoring 53 points and banking 16 rebounds in a single game. Playing in front of a sold-out crowd, Zion gave the fans something to get excited about. Within seconds of the tip-off, his teammate lobbed the ball up from just shy of the half court line and Zion took it and slammed it home, sending the fans into a fervor that didn't die down for the entire game.

Looking at Zion on the court compared to both his own teammates and his opponents, his bulk and height made him stand out, but his movement and grace anywhere on the court really made the highlight reels something to be amazed at. No matter where he was on the court, Zion was scooping up rebounds and nailing three-pointers, or even performing a behind-the-back crossover into a finger roll on a fast break. Fans went crazy, jumping out of their seats and shaking their heads in disbelief. Even when facing two defenders in the paint or sometimes three or four on a fast break, Zion showed no problems facing them and overcoming them, taking the ball to the hole every time or passing it to a teammate and finishing the play after a rebound. Coach Lee Sartor commented in an interview that Zion began each play as if it were just any other play, but by the time it was over, his finishing power could shock people to their core. The effect was similar to the way that Zion approached dunkers when he was a kid: craving more and more.

And, despite the fact that the stands would fill for hundreds that were waiting to see, talk to, and receive autographs or take pictures with Zion, he stayed himself and he stayed grateful. He is truly appreciative of his opportunities and the fact that he has become a role model for the younger kids who come to see him play. The excitement and humble showmanship that he displays on the court ignite the fans. Often times, when his highlights are shown, his face after a great play is one of joy and adrenaline, but never boastful or overly aggressive towards the other team. In this day and age, it is rare to see someone with such talent display his love and skill in such a composed way. He isn't picking on any opponent or beating his chest or yelling when he gets fouled and his shot drops, he simply flexes himself for a moment, arms down, fists clenched, maybe gives his teammates an enthusiastic high five, and then keeps on playing.

But it isn't just his on-the-court demeanor that leaves fans impressed, he even goes so far as to stay after games to sign each and every autograph and take every single selfie that any of those fans ask of him. In his post-tournament interview, Zion even reflected that this was the best tournament he had been to because of the fans. They were "electric," he said, showing him so much love and support that made this experience a memory that he would never forget even though his team didn't win the tournament.

Throughout his junior season, he received a number of honors as people recognized him for his outstanding skills. He was the MVP at the Farm Bureau Insurance Classic tournament as well as being named the Region Player of the Year for the second year in a row. MaxPreps named him the Junior of the Year and he was named to their High School All-American First Team. His name was spreading, his videos popping up on feeds across social media platforms. This was the summer where he landed on the cover of SLAM magazine. In the article that accompanied his cover shot, Adam

Figman captured the moments of awe that he felt when watching Zion live for the first time. He commented on Zion's ability to hone so much power into every single move, especially when he dunks in the middle of a game, taking on one, two, and sometimes three defenders as he pushes his way to the hole.

However, it wasn't, in fact, just the actual dunks that captured Figman's attention, though. Instead, it was the moments before and after. It was the way the whole crowd would suck in their breath as they realized they were about to see him dunk. It was the sheer jolt of energy and explosiveness that Zion exuded when pushing himself into the air, towering above the rest of the players and making it seem as if he was gliding effortlessly but determinedly towards the hoop. And then the way that the fans erupted as Zion made his way back down to the court afterward. It was as if the moment that Zion slammed the ball home, whether it was a normal dunk or windmill, he transferred that joy, that passion for the game into the people in the crowd. And it was, Figman said, something that he had never experienced before, even after covering and attending multiple NBA dunk contests. Zion's prowess on the court was beginning to rock the nation, starting right in the heart of basketball fans everywhere. He was even named to the USA Today All-USA First Team, making Zion one of the most watched high school basketball players in the country. And his year wasn't even over yet.

Moving to his AAU season, he played for the SC Supreme this year. It was on this team that he had the opportunity to face some of the other standouts in the high school basketball scene. And he didn't disappoint, living up to his stepfather's words by playing better, no matter how big the stage gets. In the Adidas Gauntlet, he went against Twenty-Two Vision, facing off against Romeo Langford, another junior who was making waves in his own way. Zion and Romeo were two of the top-ranked high school players in the country, and everyone was excited to see them battle it out. In fact, Romeo and Zion's game was being watched by a number of colleges as they dueled it out on the courts, some of which included Duke, Kansas, Indiana, South Carolina, Arkansas, Kentucky, and Clemson. Both Romeo and Zion gave the battle their all, ending with Romeo coming out on top with 28 points, four rebounds, and four assists while Zion managed 26 points and seven rebounds.

Later, Zion's team took on the Big Ballers and he faced off against LaMelo Ball, the younger brother of Los Angeles Lakers point guard Lonzo Ball. To say that the house was packed for this game was an extremely gross understatement. By the time the two walked in, the crowd was already cheering and ready for a show. Zion performed a number of pre-game dunks, everything from two-handed slams to 360s that had the crowd screaming and on the edge of their seats. The game itself was no different. Although LaMelo ended up with 36 points, 9 assists, and 6 rebounds, Zion and his SC Supreme team came out on top, Zion scoring 31 points and snagging 8 rebounds in the 104-92 point game. At the end of the AAU season, Zion ended up being named MVP of the Adidas Nations camp by averaging 22.5 points and 7.2 rebounds through only six games.

Throughout his high school career, Zion had transformed the Spartanburg community. No longer were they a region that was primarily concerned with football. He brought out and helped to develop the basketball community in his area. His mother, who worked in a neighboring town as a middle school teacher, would even get asked by her middle school students if she had heard about the basketball phenom in nearby Spartanburg. She kept her secret for a while but used it to her advantage when she promised to introduce the kids to her son, Zion, if they behaved.

The community of Spartanburg and its neighboring towns will forever be remembered as the place where Zion Williamson became a household name. His former principal even stated that it is such an odd phenomenon because typically, the way a community helps and guides a star is the story that is circulated. However, for Zion and Spartanburg, the opposite is true. Although the community supports him, he has done a lot for the area as well. His stepdad, Lee always told him to never forget that he used to be one of those little kids who was dying to see a dunk, and it shows in the way that Zion handles the love he feels from his community. When Zion goes to pick up his little brother, Noah, he gets hugged and greeted by dozens of Noah's peers, who all know how down-to-earth and approachable Zion is and how willing he is to do whatever he can to make the kids happy.

By the summer, Zion had received a scholarship offer from Mike Krzyzewski, Coach K, from Duke University, adding to the list of schools that were hopeful to have Zion in just a couple of years. One school, LSU, even offered Zion a football scholarship as well, an invitation to come and play tight end for them despite the fact that he wasn't even playing football at the time. This offer, along with the viral videos and numerous scholarship offers, only served to solidify in everyone's eyes that Zion was not just a great basketball player, he was a true athlete in every sense of the word.

CHAPTER 6: SENIOR YEAR

The hype heading into Zion's Senior year had reached a fever pitch. He had already accomplished so much, and established such a following, that many people were excited to see just what the future had in store for him. He had reached the level of being a minor celebrity with his dunks and high light videos turning him into a cultural icon.

When sportscasters and professional athletes were asked to compare Zion to someone, people were hard-pressed to choose just one person that Zion played like. Some say he has a bit of Dr. J or a little Vince Carter, but at the same time, his dynamic power and presence on the court leave many basketball fans scratching their heads. In fact, many said that he can't be compared, that his unique set of ball-handling, bulk in the paint, vertical capabilities, and grace all around the court made Zion not just "the next so-and-so," he could only be looked at as the first Zion Williamson. The director of recruiting at ESPN, Paul Biancardi, even went on to say that at this point, Zion was probably the best player in the country. And he still had a whole year of high school left.

However, life has a way of balancing itself out, and in the home opener on November 21st, Zion scored 29 points, pulled out 11 rebounds, and bruised his left foot, forcing him out for the next month of playing. He was on the sidelines and in a walking boot during this time, following the doctor's recommendations to wait until the foot was back to 100% before trying to get back out on the court.

During this time, fans and college scouts alike were disappointed due to the fact that Zion would miss the chance to play against the number one prospect in the country, RJ Barrett, who had already signed to Duke in an upcoming tournament. Even though he remained hopeful, knowing he'd be back and believing in his teammates, Zion marks this month of recovery as a big growing point for him mentally. He recognized that this was an opportunity to keep his focus on the big picture, even if it meant missing a few games in his final year of high school.

Still, when he returned in January, he showed that the injury was a temporary, inconsequential speed bump on his road to greatness. In his first game back against Asheville Christian Academy, he scored 31 points, leading his team to a 71-6 victory. A few days later, he participated in a nationally televised game at the Hoophall Classic and brought in another 36 points. On February 17th, he scored his 3,000 career point facing off against Spartanburg Christian at the regional tournament and scoring 37 points, 10 rebounds, and 5 steals.

A week later, Spartanburg Day went on to win its third consecutive regional championship, Zion adding 38 points to the scoreboard. However, when playing in the 2018 McDonald's All-American Game, Zion only played for 17 minutes, scoring eight points, before he left the game with a thumb injury and did not return.

Although his season had been affected by his two injuries, he still managed to impress a ton of people, stacking up awards and scholarship offers left and right. Zion was named South Carolina Mr. Basketball and was the runner up for Mr. Basketball USA. He was also named to the MaxPreps All-American second team and the USA Today All-USA first team.

By the end of his high school basketball career, a total of 36 colleges had offered Zion scholarships. As his stepdad was a Clemson alumnus, Lee Anderson knew that Clemson could be a prime contender for who Zion would choose to play for. Along with Clemson, Zion was primarily considering choosing between Kansas, Kentucky, North Carolina, and South Carolina. However, on January 20, 2018, on a live telecast on ESPN, Zion committed to Duke and playing for Coach K.

Looking back, both Sharonda and Lee recall their different reactions. Sharonda remembered one day when she had seen Zion get a call and take it to his room. Twenty minutes later, when she went to check on him and ask why he had been on the phone for so long, his reaction is one she remembers well. When he looked at her and told her that he was talking to Coach K, his facial expressions and body language were more those of an eager and excited teen. That call was something she knew had a lasting impact on Zion's ultimate decision to go there. After the call, Zion mentioned the way that Coach K didn't just talk about basketball, but about the brotherhood and family feel that he tried to create with his team at Duke. It turns out, this was exactly the kind of atmosphere and call that Zion was looking for.

On the other hand, after Zion committed, Lee told the Clemson coaching staff that they had had the advantage because even though Lee hadn't tried to sway Zion into choosing Clemson, he knew that Zion loved the stories that Lee had shared with him about the school growing up. When asked, Lee stated that he believed Clemson had a "mile and a half lead" over the other potential schools. However, somewhere along the way, Zion had changed his mind and was now excited to join the brotherhood and legendary coaching at Duke the following year. He would now be joining RJ Barrett and Cam Reddish as new Blue Devils. This was the first time that a team landed three of the top prospects in the same year.

CHAPTER 7: COLLEGE

When athletes move up from one stage of competition to another, there is always an odd sense of wonder that accompanies them. Nobody really knows how that person will perform at the next level of play, and often, people are wondering, will they live up to the hype or be a total bust. In Zion's case this contrast was amplified because he came from such a small town, where there weren't many strong basketball programs. This gave doubters the ammunition to say that Zion was just a big fish in a small pond.

Duke University invested heavily in their young recruits, many fans wondering if it would end up as good as the coaches and recruiters hoped. Zion Williamson did not disappoint. In his first preseason game, he ended with a double-double against Ryerson, 29 points and 13 rebounds. And that was just the beginning. Under the guidance of Coach K and with his group of "brothers" in his teammates, the Blue Devils had a pretty successful year. The Atlantic Coast Conference (ACC), the conference that Duke is in, is filled with teams like North Carolina, Louisville, Syracuse, MC State, Florida State, Notre Dame, and Clemson. In this conference, Zion would face opponents that had already proven themselves at the collegiate level, participated in the NCAA Tournament, and experienced first-hand what March Madness is all about. There are some incredibly strong contenders in the conference, so Zion would have his work cut out for him.

Weighing in at 287lbs. and measuring 6' 7" tall, Zion was still impressing the basketball community right out of the gates, playing at power forward and small forward for the Blue Devils. During the preseason, he was named on the watch list for multiple awards, including the Karl Malone Award (for power forwards), Naismith Trophy, and John R. Wooden Award. People who had been following Zion's journey since Spartanburg were excited to see how he performed on the college stage.

The electricity around the campus was electric and the whole Duke Basketball Community was excited to see what Zion would do on this new stage. When the season began, Zion scored 28 points in the first game against Kentucky, breaking the freshman debut scoring record. Duke fans, and general fans who were more specifically interested in Zion, were excited by this showing and were even more excited when it turned out that his performance was far from a fluke when he consistently performed in the next few games. Against Army, he scored 27 points, snagged 16 rebounds, and added 6 blocks to boot. And he didn't stop there.

The awards continued to pile in for Zion as the season went on. In the first week of the season, the ACC named Zion the Freshman of the Week. He ended up receiving this honor a total of five times throughout the season. Two times, he even beat out the upperclassmen in the conference and was named the ACC player of the week. He was also named the national freshman of the week, indicating that it wasn't just the ACC teams who were keeping an eye on Zion's stats. Zion also became the second player in history with 25 points, 15 rebounds, and 5 blocks in a single game. To anyone and everyone who was watching, nobody would argue that Zion Williamson wasn't living up to the hype that had followed him from Spartanburg Day.

His stellar presence on the floor continued on throughout that initial year. Zion's stepfather, Lee, must have had bittersweet feelings seeing Zion take the court against Lee's alma mater, Clemson during that freshman year. And although Zion had traded his red Spartanburg #12 jersey in for the blue and white #1 of Duke, it was not hard to spot him on the court. Even compared to the other centers and forwards, Zion's bulk made him a force to be reckoned with throughout the game. But that didn't stop him from showing his shooting ability at the three-point line or even at half court where he stole a ball from the Clemson point guard who never even saw Zion coming. Taking the ball down with a mesmerizingly powerful 360 dunk from that steal, it was clear that Zion provided an impactful fire for both his teammates and Duke fans during the game. Even though Duke ended with a loss, Zion scored 25 points and brought down 10 rebounds.

Against Syracuse on January 14, 2019, Zion continued to display his finesse and power on the court, easily splitting defenders and primarily scoring in either a driving play in the paint or by drilling free throws after being fouled. Many people who hadn't followed Zion's career in high school were amazed at just how strong this young man was, but still, he managed to sprint the court like a point guard, drive to the hole aggressively while maintaining a level of finesse in his shots that displayed his control. His ability to hang in the air and soar in from out of nowhere in order to block his opponents fired up fans and teammates alike. Duke lost in overtime, but Zion's stats showed his contributions were multi-faceted. Drilling 10 of 13 from the free throw line, he scored 35 points, 10 rebounds, and came in with four blocks, which broke the Duke record for single-game points for a freshman. Right behind his teammate RJ Barrett for ACC leaders in scoring, Zion was making his mark at the collegiate level. He was even the first freshman in Duke history to have nine 25-point games in a single season.

Of course, Zion wasn't doing it all alone. Looking back at the reason that he chose Duke in the first place, his hope for brotherhood was being fulfilled by the three other freshmen and their leader, Coach K. Also signing to Duke that year were Cam Reddish, Tre Jones, and RJ Barrett. Sportscasters everywhere were excited to see this special group of boys play, and were drilling Coach K about them early on in the season. When asked about his young players, Coach K commented on the fact that these aren't just great position players, that they are true ballplayers, able to work any position, be flexible with each other on the court, and all four of them were in it to win it. On Zion specifically, Coach K commented that Zion was the most unique player that he'd ever coached at Duke. Zion's size, his 45" vertical, his people skills, and fluidity on the court all made Zion a special kind of person. The coach also added that this group of young players meshed well with the upperclassmen, creating a true family in the team where everyone supported each other, wanted to blend their skills together, and unite for a common goal: winning games.

In an interview with all four of the freshmen, it was clear that the friendship that they had built had started early on. They had all been approached by Coach K and all knew each other from either playing against each other or watching each other at various stages throughout high school. The fact that they were all in the same year in school was just a coincidence that brought a slew of talent together in the blue and white jerseys as freshmen. Zion told the interviewer that it was initially exciting to put that jersey on, but it wasn't until later that he truly began to feel the weight and pride in it that he has now. Coach K had sat the team down and talked to them for a few hours about Duke. He listed the school's values, talked about the reputation of the team, and let the young men know exactly what it is that they were doing when they placed that Duke name on. They weren't just out there to play and win, they were there to do it while upholding the values and tradition of Duke's illustrious school and program.

However, Zion's initial year in college was not without its complications. During the game against North Carolina, Zion suffered from a shoe blowout. It was one of the most talked about moments of the season in the basketball world, videos of the incident going viral and Nike's stock dropping a total of $1.1 billion dollars afterward. In a play where Zion was attempting to plant his left foot and push back off to go in the other direction, the sole of Zion's left foot hit the wood and the force of his foot carried through, separating the sole from the body of the shoe. Zion's whole left foot is seen going through this separation, leaving the shoe hanging awkwardly from Zion's ankle as he fell to the floor, his right knee twisting at the lack of support and continuing momentum that went into the move. He crumpled to the floor, immediately clutching his right knee and managed to hobble off the court, remove the shoes, and head to the locker room to get checked out. Video clips and shots of the blown-out shoe quickly spread across the internet, raising questions about the shoe industry and college sponsorship programs like never before.

The school has a Nike contract, so athletes, like Zion, are required to wear the Nike shoes for games, sport the Nike logo on other apparel, and more. Some people used this as a prime example to question the validity in forcing athletes to do that based on a sponsorship decision made by the school. Others brought up the fact that athletes who play for their college, like Zion, don't make any money for playing and being sponsored. They are basically earning money for the school, for the NCAA, and for Nike.

Beyond the normal amateur arguments, there were also other's who were more worried about Zion's future. There were those around him that cautioned Zion, telling him that if he continued to play college ball, he might risk more injuries like this and miss his shot at the pros. Some argued that this was less an issue with Nike and more of a direct display of the fact that Zion Williamson is not the "normal" basketball player that Nike had developed shoes for. It isn't every day that a 6'7" 285lb. athlete is not only wearing those shoes but doing so and moving in the way that Zion does. Supporters of the fact that Zion can't truly be compared to anyone before him are mostly in agreement that this shoe blow out just went on to support the fact that Zion was in a class of his own, and that not even Nike could have anticipated the wear and tear that a person like him would place on the shoes. Either way, this blowout resulted in a Grade 1 knee sprain, and Zion would sit the final six games of the regular season out while he recovered.

By the time he returned, Duke was nearing the end of the ACC Tournament. Rejoining his teammates on the court for the quarterfinals against Syracuse, Zion showed the world that the knee sprain, like his bruised foot from high school, was nothing that anybody needed to worry about anymore. His first game back, he set a school record and tied the ACC record, going 13 for 13 for a total of 29 points. He also brought in 14 rebounds and 5 steals, erasing any concerns with his great performance. In one play, Zion stole the ball from the Syracuse guard near the half court line. By the time he approached his own three-point line, Zion picked up his dribble, took his two steps, and then soared through the air from just past the free-throw line and slammed it home. And this happened within the first three minutes of the game, igniting the fans, and pumping up Zion and his teammates.

He went on to play in the semi-finals against North Carolina again. He scored 31 points, including the game-winner that sent Duke to the championship. Driving to the hole with only 30 seconds left to play, Zion went face to face against the defenders, a second sliding over to try and stop the force that is Zion Williamson. Tossing it up, Zion's shot kissed the glass before bouncing off of the rim, but Zion was there in a flash, like his feet had never even hit the ground, and he was able to tip it in, bringing the Blue Devils up 74-73 in what would be the last score of the game.

In the finals, Duke faced off against Florida State, Zion contributing 21 points as the Blue Devils went on to win the whole tournament. Even though he came in late, Zion was named the ACC Tournament MVP, only the 6th freshman ever to win it. He also scored a total of 81 points in just three games, breaking the record for Duke that had been set back in 1961 by Art Heyman who scored 80 points in the same number of games. Additionally, Zion surpassed the last freshman three-game record of 78 points that had been achieved by North Carolina's Phil Ford in 1975. Zion and his teammates were at the top of their game as they headed into March Madness, hunting for another championship title, this time in the NCAA tournament.

CHAPTER 8: MARCH MADNESS

There is something special about March on college campuses. Every team that makes the tournament knows the world's eyes are on them and their feats will go down in the memories of their fans for a lifetime. Perhaps nowhere is this more true than at Duke University. Duke's history and fans are without a parallel. To say this would be a different experience than the State Tournament's a Spartanburg Country Day would be a bit of an understatement.

Favored by many to make the Final Four, and by about 35% of people to take the whole thing, Duke was debuting as the first seed for the East in the tournament against the 16th seed, North Dakota State University. Zion had been the talk of the season, drawing in celebrities like Barack Obama and Jay-Z to come and watch his explosive dunks and graceful power on the court. Obama even reportedly had Duke on his bracket to take the title.

Capitalizing on the fandom, interest, and viewership that came along with Zion, CBS created a special "Zion Cam" that would be solely focused on following Zion's every move on the court, including a specially hired person to shoot video and capture audio of Zion throughout the tournament. One CBS producer mentioned that this was something that had never been done to this degree before, but completely understood that Zion represented a unique talent that nobody had ever seen before, so of course, CBS provided a unique solution for fans at home that would be anxious to see Zion's every move.

Duke started the tournament off strong, taking care of North Dakota State before moving on to face the #9 seed, University of Central Florida, UCF. In both games, Zion was seen flying across the court both when he swatted away shots and passes from the other teams and when he was making his way to the rim. In the third round, Duke's young team faced off against Virginia Tech.

In both the second and third rounds, Duke had beat its opponents by only one or two points respectively. But Zion and his brothers on the team were still in the hunt for the title, Zion doing whatever he could to put points up for his team and lead them on their way there. Then, they came up against the number two seeded Michigan State in the Elite Eight. Emotions ran high as the Blue Devils faced the pressure of the Spartan team. The flexibility of the young Duke team came in handy as they battled for the chance to advance. Zion was drilling three-pointers and posting up in the paint as well. In the end, though, it wasn't enough as the Michigan State team advanced after beating the Duke boys by one point. It was a heartbreaking loss for the team, but a great set of memories for Zion and his teammates.

By the end of that season, Zion had gone through a lot. He'd suffered an injury and bounced back, dealt with the disappointment of losing in the regional finals during March Madness, and was becoming acclimated to life as a college student-athlete. He had played in a total of 33 games for Duke that season, averaging 22.6 points per game, many of them the passionate and powerful dunks that so many people admired about Zion's gameplay. He also averaged 8.9 rebounds a game, 2.1 steals, and 1.8 blocks. Overall, he shot 68% from the field and did pretty well from both the key and the perimeter. In fact, he had the top shot percentage in the ACC and the second highest in the NCAA, and he had missed six games due to his injury. His shot percentage was the highest ever for a freshman and the publicity and exuberance that he showed every time he was on the court had droves of fans, new and old, hanging on his every move. Zion was also one of only three players to ever have 500 points, 50 steals, and 50 blocks in their freshman year. This put him in the same group as Kevin Durant, who played at Texas and is now a Golden State Warrior, and Anthony Davis, former Kentucky player now playing for the New Orleans Pelicans. Zion was named the NCAA Player of the Year as well as the Rookie of the Year, fulfilling his childhood goal of being the best in the nation at the college level. Additionally, he was honored as the Sporting New Player of the Year and Freshman of the Year. As a freshman, he was a force to be reckoned with and many people were anxious to see what he would do next.

CHAPTER 9: STEPPING ON THE WORLD'S BIGGEST STAGE

Looking to the future, Zion decided that after playing for Duke as a freshman, his next move led directly to the NBA. On April 15, 2019, Zion declared eligibility for the 2019 NBA draft. Lee Anderson, his stepdad, solidified the fact that Zion would not be returning to Duke for his sophomore year. Zion is joined in the draft by fellow Blue Devils Cam Reddish and RJ Barrett who are expected to go high in the draft as well.

After the Draft Lottery, the New Orleans Pelicans won the first pick overall, and Zion is pretty much guaranteed to go at that slot. Teammates RJ and Cam are predicted to go in the first ten picks as well. Many in the basketball community are excited to see Zion as he may come across some of the very players that people are trying to compare him to such as Lebron James.

Another question that many fans are left wondering is what position Zion will play since the caliber of play is going to be upped on him once more. Going from high school ball to college and then to the pros within the course three years seems like a huge jump, and people are not sure if Zion will live up to the hype as many in the past who were highly touted before the NBA never actually panned out on the professional court. Not only will Zion be facing much older and experienced players, but he may also be more restricted to the position that he will play depending on the coaching staff and the established members on the team. This may lead to a change in Zion's style, but fans should rest assured that no matter what happens, Zion's enthusiasm and energy will always be present any time he laces up and gets out there. Lee sticks to his earlier prediction that the bigger the stage, the better Zion will get.

Although he's come a long way from the little boy that used to wake up at 5am to practice his ball handling skills and workout with his stepdad, his family is still as present as ever. Sharonda, his mother, lets anyone who asks know that despite the fact that he's made headline news and is looking at joining the largest stage available for a basketball player, he's still just a down to earth kid who loves to be a homebody whenever he gets the chance. Spending time with his stepbrother Noah (who likes to steal the spotlight by sleeping on camera during big events), eating food from his parent's house, and just watching TV and hanging out with family are some of the things that Sharonda sees when she looks at Zion. She and the rest of her family may be the only ones left that look at Zion and don't attach him automatically to a basketball jersey and a fierce expression of adrenaline after one of his ever-popular dunks, but one thing is for sure, both his family and the world will be hanging on the edge of their seats to see where life and basketball take Zion Williamson next.

MORE FROM JACKSON CARTER BIOGRAPHIES

My goal is to spark the love of reading in young adults around the world. Too often children grow up thinking they hate reading because they are forced to read material they don't care about. To counter this we offer accessible, easy to read biographies about sportspeople that will give young adults the chance to fall in love with reading.

Go to the Website Below to Join Our Community

https://mailchi.mp/7cced1339ff6/jcbcommunity

Or Find Us on Facebook at

www.facebook.com/JacksonCarterBiographies

As a Member of Our Community You Will Receive:

First Notice of Newly Published Titles

Exclusive Discounts and Offers

Influence on the Next Book Topics

Don't miss out, join today and help spread the love of reading around the world!

OTHER WORKS BY JACKSON CARTER BIOGRAPHIES

Patrick Mahomes: The Amazing Story of How Patrick Mahomes Became the MVP of the NFL

Donovan Mitchell: How Donovan Mitchell Became a Star for the Salt Lake City Jazz

Luka Doncic: The Complete Story of How Luka Doncic Became the NBA's Newest Star

The Eagle: Khabib Nurmagomedov: How Khabib Became the Top MMA Fighter and Dominated the UFC

Lamar Jackson: The Inspirational Story of How One Quarterback Redefined the Position and Became the Most Explosive Player in the NFL

Jimmy Garoppolo: The Amazing Story of How One Quarterback Climbed the Ranks to Be One of the Top Quarterbacks in the NFL

Zion Williamson: The Inspirational Story of How Zion Williamson Became the NBA's First Draft Pick

Kyler Murray: The Inspirational Story of How Kyler Murray Became the NFL's First Draft Pick

Do Your Job: The Leadership Principles that Bill Belichick and the New England Patriots Have Used to Become the Best Dynasty in the NFL

Turn Your Gaming Into a Career Through Twitch and Other Streaming Sites: How to Start, Develop and Sustain an Online Streaming Business that Makes Money

From Beginner to Pro: How to Become a Notary Public

Made in the USA
Las Vegas, NV
25 July 2021